the ART of FOOD presentation
the eye also eats

DORIS MOSS

Cover design, interior book design, and eBook design
by Blue Harvest Creative
www.blueharvestcreative.com

All photographs provided by and copyright © 2016 Doris Moss

THE ART OF FOOD PRESENTATION

Copyright © 2016 Doris Moss

All rights reserved. Except as permitted under the U.S. Copyright Act of 1976, no part of this publication may be reproduced, distributed, or transmitted in any form or by any means, or stored in a database or retrieval system, without prior written permission of the publisher.

ISBN-13: 978-1533311955
ISBN-10: 1533311951

TABLE OF CONTENTS
the art of food presentation

PROLOGUE..5

CHAPTER ONE: AN INTRODUCTION TO FOOD DECORATION............7

    Peach Pinwheels..8
    Pinwheel With Grape Flowers...9
    Melon Balls and Spirals...10
    Apricots and Spirals..10
    Cottage Cheese Salad..11
    Pineapple Stars and Mandarin Pinwheels.................................11
    All Fruit Salad..12
    Carrot Raisin Salad..12
    Melon Wedges..13
    Split Pineapple...14
    Watermelon Basket..14
    Waldorf Salad..15
    Gelatin with Prunes..16

CHAPTER TWO: APPETIZERS (HORS D'OEUVRES)........................17

    Shrimp and Pineapple Trees...17
    Cheese Mouse..18
    Cheese House...19
    Deviled Eggs..20
    Assorted Appetizer Platters..21
    Special Appetizers...22

CHAPTER THREE: THE SALAD BAR..24

    Pale Potato Salad...24
    Sliced Radish Flowers..25
    Poppies..26
    Star Flowers...27
    Rose...27
    Rose Variation...28
    Mushrooms..28
    Macaroni Salads..29
    Cole Slaw Salad...30

Marinated Green Bean Salad..31
Pea Salad..31
Herring Salad..32
Meat Salad...33
Celery Salad..34
Beet Salad..35
Spaghetti Salad...36

CHAPTER FOUR: MAIN COURSES..................................37

Glazed Ham Dish...37
The Garnished Tongue..38
The Tuna Dish..39
Cold Salmon Platter...40
Trays of Cheeses and Cold Cuts..40
Delicatessen Assortment...41
Cold Open-faced Sandwiches..41
Hot Open-faced Sandwiches..42

CHAPTER FIVE: ESPECIALLY FOR CHILDREN................43

The Vegetable Platter...43
Smiley...44
The Little Bread House...45
The Lady Bugs..45
The Penguins..46

CHAPTER SIX: HOLIDAY ENSEMBLES..............................47

Rainbow Gelatin Layer Dessert..47
Funny Faces..48
Rollmops..48
King Neptune's New Year Salad..49
Easter Ensemble...49
Glazed Ham Chaud-froid...50
Ambrosia Salad..51
Festive Shrimp Salad...51
Christmas Fruit Tray...51
Molded Strawberry Gelatin Dessert..52
Vegetable Flower Bouquet Centerpieces..52

ABOUT THE AUTHOR..55

PROLOGUE
an introduction to food decoration

This book is the summation of experiences resulting from many years of preparing and decorating tantalizing dishes for banquets, parties, and events presented for distinguished crowds in renown hotels and restaurants. The theme of this book revolves around the issue, "how important is the sight of a dish or the presentation of food for the enjoyment of the diner?" It reflects most succinctly the deep rooted conviction of the author in a well-known belief in her native Germany "Das auge isst mit", meaning the aesthetic sight of food is a very important aspect of the dining experience.

Ms. Moss weaves her presentations around her conviction and applies it in the preparation of every single dish throughout the book. For her the sight of the offered food is as important as the taste and it adds a tremendous amount of delight to the diner's epicurean experience. She also strongly believes than an artfully decorated dish does not only tantalize the appetite of the person but also initiates a good relationship between the hostess and the guest. She argues that just as we are conscious of the aesthetic discrimination of the eye when we dress up or decorate our homes we ought to be equally critical when we serve food; to stimulate the imagination of the diner is to sweeten his/her anticipation of a worthy experience, in doing so the mutual satisfaction between the host and the guest is satisfactorily enhanced.

DORIS MOSS

the art of food presentation

The second strong statement this book makes is that the creation of a well presented dish is not necessarily the domain of a well-trained, or renown chef. An ordinary cook or a housewife who throws a party will be as well equipped to present a well-decorated dish if she learns how to utilize the ordinary ingredients that are already present in her kitchen.

Decorating food is not new. This book retains some decorating techniques and ideas that have been part of the culinary tradition. Flower and petal decorations on the white icing of a wedding cake, or the gingerbread man of the western culture are traditional examples. Among the multitudinous cook books which are found on the market very few address the art of decorating or food presentation techniques per se. Some works suggest decoration by their titles but they are in fact recipe books in disguise. Others list various utensils commonly used and basic food items to be used in decorating and provide vague generalities on how the tools and food items combine to make any specific piece of food decorations. The author's mode of presentation, however, is distinctly different. She focuses on decorating the specific dish step by step and explains how to cut a certain food item or how to smooth a pie surface with utmost detail and accuracy in a very simple language.

This book is designed for individuals who are interested to present a well-groomed and appetizing table to entertain their families and friends. This is not to say that professionals won't find these ideas interesting. Ms. Moss has applied these techniques at her own job preparing buffets. The enthusiastic reception of the patrons and compliments of the guests have prompted her to write this book, thus filling a gap in the contemporary literature of culinary art.

CHAPTER ONE

an introduction to food decoration

According to culinary tradition there are certain rules to follow for food decoration or garniture. All food decoration or garniture must be edible. We have occasion in this book to make use of toothpicks for fastening. We do not use wires or other inedible fasteners other than those toothpicks. We do not decorate or garnish with confection or artificial colors. Items used for decoration ought to blend tastefully with the main ingredients. The correct purpose of the decoration is to enhance attraction for a dish, not to upstage and cause distraction from it.

The art of food decoration is applicable to all courses of dining and for a variety of beneficiaries. In this chapter we will illustrate our theme with some elementary examples which require no cooking. In subsequent chapters we will continue to feature mostly cold dishes for two reasons. Hot, steaming dishes are seldom suitable for our craft. Heat may have an adverse effect on most of our decorative ideas except for bright garniture that may be sprinkles. The other reason is that by putting emphasis on dishes that could be prepared in advance, we are providing the reader with a repertoire from which one can single-handedly prepare sufficient volume for a number of guests. When you are confident of your skills at decorating, I doubt that you would want your immediate family to be the only beneficiaries of your art. Singles may find in this book a brand new incentive to entertain their friends. Don't forget that a hot entree could also be a nucleus around which you may place several decorative, previously prepared cold dishes.

CHAPTER TWO will be of special interest to those who wish to embellish their dinners with hors d'oeuvres or to host cocktail parties.

CHAPTER THREE is a vast salad bar, a result of much experience I have had preparing salads for the busy buffets of large hotels. Any one or group of these decorated salads you may want to select for your family dinner or for a large party. It is noteworthy that it is feasible for you to prepare every one of these salads single-handedly within a few hours for a special occasion.

In **CHAPTER FOUR**, we will show how to decorate meat. Usually the meat is cooked in advance and cool when the decoration is applied. You will find a couple of exciting and exotic displays in this chapter.

Children and their tastes receive our special attention in **CHAPTER FIVE**. However, the young at heart need not feel excluded.

Finally, in **CHAPTER SIX** some ensembles with full decor of holiday themes are suggested for your pleasure.

You probably already possess in your kitchen most of the necessary utensils for the ideas of this book. You might consider acquiring a melon-ball cutter and a pastry bag and tube. These simple devices give a finer effect for some decoration. A restaurant supply business is probably the first place to look for the pastry bag and tube.

DORIS MOSS
the art of food presentation

We believe that the major benefit to be obtained from this book is that it will stimulate your own creativity. By learning the examples in this book you will be armed with a brilliant repertoire, but an infinitely greater one may be unlocked from your imagination. You won't be flunking any chef school by going your own way at home. The few traditional culinary rules mentioned above merely serve to protect the wholesomeness of food decoration. By at least following the tradition of "The Art of Food Decorating" you will be adding a new dimension to the pleasures of eating for those you care for, and you will be resurrecting a neglected art.

To illustrate our approach of presenting food more attractively we will begin with some very elementary examples. Here and throughout the book blank surfaces receive bright colors and bright surfaces receive contrasting bright colors. Be judicious on how much decoration you apply to a surface. The effect of too many garnishes is similar to the effect of wearing too much make-up. Remember that the purpose is to embellish and not to distract from the main ingredients; for example, because of their naturally bright colors to contrast with the main body, the best material for the decoration of a bowl of cottage cheese is fruit. And what more could one ask for nutrition than this team? The cottage cheese in the bowl should be smoothed with a spatula or a knife. The cheese may have a flat surface or rise slightly in a mound with no difference to the chosen decoration. Our first example, the peach pinwheels, is made from canned peach halves.

PEACH PINWHEELS

CHAPTER ONE
an introduction to food decoration

The halves are preferable to canned slices because the canned peaches are usually not sliced evenly. slice them evenly yourself. Each pinwheel revolves around a maraschino cherry; substitute fresh strawberries for the cherries when the season allows. Parsley or mint gives an excellent contrast of color.

PINWHEEL WITH GRAPE FLOWERS

With a minimum of effort a striking variation of the first example can be made. Place one peach pinwheel in the center and surround it with green grape flowers each of which is composed of six grape petals around a maraschino cherry. Peach slices may line the rim if the bowl is large enough otherwise avoid overloading the cottage cheese canvas.

Another variation can be as follows: with a melon-ball cutter make balls of cantaloupe and watermelon, which shall alternate around the rim. Inside of these you may make a ring of alternating green grapes and little spirals of whip cream applied by a pastry bag and tube.

PINWHEEL VARIATIONS

For a variation of the above description, line the rim with halved apricots with their pits facing down. Inside of the apricots is a ring of alternating maraschino cherries and whip cream spirals applied by a pastry bag and tube.

DORIS MOSS
the art of food presentation

MELON BALLS AND SPIRALS

In the next example we place halved apricots facing upward, each with a maraschino cherry in its pit. A ring of these crowned apricot halves alternating with canned prunes circles the rim.

APRICOTS AND SPIRALS

CHAPTER ONE
an introduction to food decoration

COTTAGE CHEESE SALAD

Use the following recipe for a cottage cheese salad.

- One pint of small curd cottage cheese
- One pint of whipped cream (non-dairy or real)
- One three-ounce package of gelatin dessert
- One eleven-ounce can of mandarin orange sections
- One eight-ounce can of crushed pineapple

Drain the mandarins well before mixing them with all of the other ingredients in a bowl. Cool the salad in the refrigerator. The flavor of the gelatin dessert you select may affect the color of the salad. In the illustration a red gelatin dessert caused a pink hue. Four stars of quartered pineapple rings and four pinwheels of mandarins made as described in the previous example alternate in a circle around the salad. Maraschino cherries are in the center of each star and pinwheel. Green grapes have been added for contrast linking each pinwheel to each star.

PINEAPPLE STARS AND MANDARIN PINWHEELS

The example above is constructed from quartered pineapple rings and sections of mandarin orange. Five pineapple quarters make a five-point pineapple star. Five sections of mandarin orange make a mandarin pinwheel. Three stars and three pinwheels alternate in a circle. Each has a fresh berry or maraschino cherry in its center.

DORIS MOSS
the art of food presentation

ALL FRUIT SALAD

Fruit alone in a bowl may be arranged to make a very attractive pattern. Canned pineapple rings, apricots, prunes, green grapes, and maraschino cherries comprise an arabesque. For such a salad you will want to drain some but not all of the juices packed with the canned fruit. This salad may be especially good on hot summer days.

CARROT RAISIN SALAD

Another good salad for simple decorations is a shredded carrot salad.

- Mix one measure of raisins with every four measures of shredded carrots
- Add a teaspoon of white vinegar, sugar to taste, and enough mayonnaise to moisten
- Sprinkle coconut flakes all over the top

The carrot salad is decorated by halved pineapple rings perpendicular to the rim alternating with maraschino cherries. An alternative to this is a ring of alternating prunes and mounds of whipped cream applied by a pastry bag and tube topped with maraschino cherries.

CHAPTER ONE
an introduction to food decoration

MELON WEDGES

Nature may provide its own containers for fruit salads. By removing the top one third of a honey dew melon you may create the illusion that it is a container for grapes. Remove the seeds from the surface area of the melon but leave the meat. The top should be carved in a zigzag fashion. Green and purple grapes then rest on the top. Cut serving size wedges of cantaloupe and watermelon to alternate in a circle around the honey dew. Make plenty of wedges to fill the tray; and with clusters of green grapes avoid allowing any open spaces. Grapevine leaves make a nice surrounding if available.

SPLIT PINEAPPLE

Cut a fresh pineapple in halves from top to bottom including the leaves. Scoop out all of the meat and cut it in chunks. Remove the tough center portions also. Fill the pineapple halves with chunks of its own meat, black and green grapes, fresh strawberries, chunks of fresh peach, or any fresh fruit which you desire. Place a mint leaf on top of the fruit collection. The pineapple halves will face opposite directions on your serving platter and the two empty spaces may be filled by two halves of a grapefruit facing upward. Both grapefruit halves may be garnished with a fresh strawberry dividing two mint leaves. Once this platter is served, ice cubes may be placed here and there to keep the fruit chilled.

WATERMELON BASKET

A watermelon basket is an impressive presentation well known in the food business and mentioned in other books. By taking precautions not to break the handle you may easily make your own. The problem is that the handle might break from stress while you are cutting off the rest of the top. I suggest that you start your carving at the angles where the handle and the zigzag rim will meet. Give the handle no less than two inches of width. Of course one must never lift the watermelon basket by the handle. Scoop out all of the seeds and meat. The top of the basket is filled with balls of cantaloupe and watermelon cut by a melon-ball cutter. Also there are green grapes, mint leaves, and coconut flakes. Underneath these, however, the basket is filled by assorted melon chunks.

CHAPTER ONE
an introduction to food decoration

WALDORF SALAD

A salad may become a dessert due to elementary decorating technique. Here is a Waldorf salad which enjoys such a conversion.

To make a Waldorf salad

- Peel and slice red delicious apples which are ripe
- Mix them with mayonnaise, chopped nuts, diced celery hearts, and a dash of salt

The celery hearts are chosen for this salad because they are more tender than the stalks. Finely chopped nuts form a ring around the edge of the salad. Thin slices of apple, fresh whipped cream applied by pastry bag and tube, and maraschino cherries combine to make a decorative design as shown by the illustration. Imitation whipped cream is not as satisfactory for such decorations as it tends to lose its mold soon after it is applied.

DORIS MOSS
the art of food presentation

GELATIN WITH PRUNES

A decorative combination of fruit and gelatin dessert is our last example.

- Dissolve two six-ounce packages of orange flavored gelatin dessert in three cups of boiling water
- Add eight cups of ice cubes and stir until gelatin thickens
- Remove any ice not yet melted and pour one inch of the gelatin mixture into a round mold
- Chill it until it has thickened but is not yet firm
- Gently add the remainder of the gelatin mixture and chill again until it is all firm
- A whipped cream trimming may be added for decoration. Fruit is generally the best garnish for gelatin desserts and a variety of molds can stimulate many creative ideas.

CHAPTER TWO

appetizers (hors d'ouerves)

If you have been reluctant to include appetizers with your entertainment because of their difficulty to prepare or expense, this chapter will put you at ease. One need only to contrast the following suggestions with a pile of potato chips to realize that the greater appeal is given when the home made appetizers are served. All ingredients included in this chapter are usually obtainable at a supermarket or in some instances in a delicatessen.

Although very simple, our first two preparations will make a pleasant impression upon your guests as well as to stimulate their appetites. To a head of cabbage of medium size attach with toothpicks shrimps which are cooked, shelled and cleaned. Crown the cabbage with parsley for maximum color contrast against the shrimps. The shrimp tree ought to rest on a bed of ice to retard spoiling during its presentation. I recommend that cocktail sauce, preferably in glassware, accompany the shrimp tree.

SHRIMP AND PINEAPPLE TREES

DORIS MOSS
the art of food presentation

For another variation use some fruits with cheese on the center of your platter and surround it with assorted cheese cubes. Put the fruits on the center of your platter and surround it with assorted cheese cubes. Keep plenty of toothpicks nearby. You can also decide to use a pineapple tree, the pineapple may be the source of a delicious dessert for later in the evening.

CHEESE MOUSE

The mouse will mix well with any crackers and any wine you may have chosen for the occasion. The basic ingredients are as follows:

- One eight-ounce package of cream cheese
- One jar of Roka Blue
- One jar of Old English
- One small onion chopped
- One tablespoon of Worcestershire sauce
- Chopped parsley
- Chopped pecans or walnuts

Mix the first six of the listed ingredients with a fork. Mold the rough shape of the body of your mouse and roll it in the chopped nuts. Work on the pointed nose and other desired features. Two crackers cut into halves form ears. The crackers are divided so that they may be placed at angles for better effect. Two black olives are the eyes; parsley stems are the whiskers. The tail is constructed of black live peels.

CHAPTER TWO
appetizers (hors d'ouerves)

CHEESE HOUSE

As the illustration shows, a parade of cheese balls files by the cheese house. these are a variety of exquisite little appetizers which I shall describe in their order of appearance away from the toothpick stand.

Bavarian Cheese Balls

Mix cream cheese with Parmesan cheese. Form small balls from this mixture and roll them in crumbled pumpernickel.

Sweet Cheese Kisses

Mix cream cheese with chopped maraschino cherries and then form balls.

Surprise Marbles

Season cream cheese with salt and pepper. Form balls and insert one half of a walnut into each. Roll the balls in finely chopped parsley.

DORIS MOSS
the art of food presentation

Spicy Cheese Balls

Add finely chopped onion to cream cheese. Season with salt and pepper. Form balls and roll them in paprika.

The last type of cheese balls is made from the same recipe as the one used to make the cheese mouse.

The walls of the cheese house are constructed of four slabs of either Monterey jack cheese or Muenster cheese. Butter is spread on the outside wall and edges of each slab to fasten the pretzels and to glue the four walls together. For this purpose butter is preferable to margarine. If you do not wish to make so many of the special cheese balls as to fill the house, assorted cheese chunks may fill the house underneath a top layer of the assorted balls. Avoid jolting your cheese house; it does not meet with F.H.A. standards.

APPETIZER (HORS D'OUERVES) PLATTERS

Up to this point in this chapter I have been sharing with you some original, but very practicable ideas from my repertoire. there is of course a different class of hors d'oeuvres which to the minds of many is nearer to the standard idea of what an hors d'oeuvres display is expected to look like. Such a presentation consists of assorted bite size creations, often colorful and exotic, on a platter to be served with cocktails. So, to start you on the road to expertise at making hors d'oeuvres both creative and conventional, you need only follow the easy instructions for the following three platters.

DEVILED EGGS

CHAPTER TWO
appetizers (hors d'ouerves)

Deviled eggs are an old standard seemingly included in all books that give instructions for hors d'oeuvres. Nevertheless, they are an excellent and inexpensive choice if you haven't the time for more elaborate work. Furthermore, they may prove to be a refreshing variation of egg for your family. As follows:

- Hard boil one dozen eggs
- One quarter cup of mayonnaise
- Two tablespoons of prepared mustard
- Some drops of Tabasco sauce
- Salt and pepper to taste

Cut in half-lengthwise each of the hard-boiled eggs. Carefully remove the yolks; we do not want the whites broken. Press the yolks through a fine sieve. Mix this yolk with the above mixture. Refill the egg whites with a pastry tube.

There are several ways to decorate the naturally bright yellow and white of your deviled eggs. The theme ought to be bright contrast. Pimento and black olive skin cut into heart and star shapes, respectively, is one idea if you have mold cutters. Without the special cutters you may cut them both into diamond shapes with a sharp knife. Parsley should go well with the deviled eggs or perhaps have a shrimp resting on top of the yolk mixture. Arrange the eggs attractively on the platter or try. Probably a circular pattern is preferable for a round platter; perhaps an oval, egg-like pattern on a rectangular tray.

ASSORTED APPETIZER (HORS D'OUERVES) PLATTERS

DORIS MOSS

the art of food presentation

A single file of deviled eggs is the nucleus of our colorful assorted hors d'oeuvres platter. Flanking the deviled eggs are pieces of buttered toast which are prepared as specified below, then quartered evenly and relieved of their crusts. On one side of the deviled eggs these bite sized squares of toast are completely covered by anchovies with a strip of pimento laid across the center. On the other side of the eggs two small sardines with head and tail opposite are laid on each piece of toast. Each pair of sardines is in turn topped with chives and a pearl onion.

To the outside of the anchovy treat are spirals. These are made from two slices of cold cut luncheon meat style of cooked salami on, both of which is spread cream cheese. The covered slices are joined and rolled and then refrigerated until they stiffen for easier slicing. Thin slices from the spiral rolls are put on top of round crackers.

To the outside of the sardines are two rows of delicious spreads. For the first of these mix chives into cream cheese. All salt and pepper to taste. Apply this spread on to round crackers with a pastry bag and tube and decorated with paprika. The next spread is a mixture of one-half cream cheese and one-half lox mixed first in a blender and then applied to slices of cocktail rye bread in a fashion indicated by the illustration with a pastry bag and tube.

On the other end of the platter is a row of celery stalks alternately stuffed with Roka blue and Old English applied by a pastry bag and tube. Next to the celery is a simple example of narrow pieces of toast without crust covered by a luncheon spread and topped with slices of green stuffed olive.

The interior line of deviled eggs stretches diagonally to connect two corners of the platter. Thus, it is the longest line and each line of hors d'oeuvres away from it becomes shorter and shorter. The remaining two corners may well be filled by salami hats. For each salami hat make a conical shape with a slice of salami and fill it with a stuffed green olive fastened with a toothpick.

SPECIAL APPETIZERS

CHAPTER TWO
appetizers (hors d'ouerves)

I believe I can already feel your growing confidence at the thought of hosting parties. If you are not equipped with a fancy serving tray or platter, or if you need more than you possess, remember that you may substitute a mirror for such pieces. This is a very acceptable practice and is done by professionals. Here is one more platter relatively more advanced than those preceding. It should establish your reputation as and expert.

On the outside are cheese balls similar to those we have seen before. For these mix cream cheese, onion salt, and pepper. Form the balls and roll them in finely chopped walnuts or pecans. Insert toothpicks.

Inside of the cheese balls is caviar toast. Spread caviar, real or imitation, on lightly buttered toast with crusts removed. Cut each toast to make four triangles and top each triangle with half of a pearl onion. Nestled between the triangles of caviar toast on one side are smoked salmon cones. Cut the smoked salmon to make a square slice. Roll this slice to make a cone. Soften cream cheese at room temperature with a little milk. Stuff the salmon cone with the cream cheese through a pastry bag and tube. For this delicate hors d'oeuvre you may wish to apply a clear glaze to preserve its freshness and bright appearance. To prepare the clear glaze dissolve one envelope of unflavored gelatin in one-half cup of cold water. Add one cup of hot water. Nestled between the triangles of caviar toast on the other side are prosciutto rolls. Each of these is a very fine slice of prosciutto ham wrapped around a strip of melon and fastened by a toothpick. The prosciutto rolls may also need a clear glaze.

Close to the center are two rows of stuffed cherry tomatoes. From the top of each cherry tomato cut downward three times near the edges without cutting all of the way through. The remaining uncut portion in the center will look like a triangle from the top. This center portion is removed with thumb and forefinger. A blossom remains. Remove the seeds and fill the blossom with the deviled egg mixture given above.

Crowned cucumbers occupy the center. Mix in a blender drained tuna, mayonnaise, cream cheese, and onion salt. Cut fresh cucumber in slices one-half inch thick. Apply tuna mixture on to the cucumber slices with a pastry bag and tube or a melon-ball cutter. Top the center of the spread with capers.

CHAPTER THREE
the salad bar

There are several reasons why your salads need not be mere side shows. Those who are among the growing number of people who are interested in a vegetarian diet are bound to focus their attention on salads. Their nutritional assets make them distinct and indispensable whether or not one is a vegetarian. Salads provide more good food for your money than any other type of serving; that is a fact not to be taken too lightly nowadays. You will learn from this chapter that it is possible for you to single-handedly prepare a lavish buffet for numerous guests if a salad bar is the foundation and gets the emphasis. Lastly, and especially for the purpose of this book, salads can be marvelously decorated.

Creating a salad bar is one way to put the accent on salads and to show off your skills at decoration. It allows you to host many guests with dishes appealing to their sight as well as to their taste. Any number of the salads given below could be prepared by you within a few hours of the arrival of your guests. While the salads are refrigerated briefly to preserve their freshness, you may be preparing your special hot entree during the last minutes before your friends arrive.

IMAGINATIVE SALADS

Here are two ways for giving some extra decoration to assembly of salads. They can be placed between the bowls. Make a palm tree from a tall, slender carrot with a greet pepper top. The pepper should be appropriately trimmed for looks. Green leaves from a pineapple may be substituted for the pepper. Both pepper or leaves would be attached to the carrot by a toothpick. make two identical fruit pyramids by halving one grapefruit, one red apple, one lemon, and a lime. Carve each half of a fruit to make a crown shape. There is no need to scrape out the meat. Place each half on top of another from the bottom to the top in the order by which they are listed above. A whole cherry tomato sits on top of the lime. Skewer the two pyramids from the top.

Never fail to decorate what you intend to serve. I hope that the ideas I give in this chapter for several popular salads shall inspire your creativity. I have used original ideas including some variations of the circular trim theme we used in chapter one.

POTATO SALADS

The pale potato salad is a good canvas for flower artwork. The first six of the following examples are from our potato salad garden. In case you are interested I include my favorite recipe for the salad.

- Two pounds of boiled potatoes peeled and sliced
- Two hard-boiled eggs chopped
- One-half cup of chopped onion
- One-half cup of chopped dill pickle
- One cup of mayonnaise
- One tablespoon of prepared mustard
- One-quarter cup of chopped parsley
- One tablespoon of sugar
- Two tablespoons of white vinegar
- One tablespoon of chopped pimento
- Crumbled bits from five strips of crisp fried bacon
- Salt and pepper to taste

Combine all of the ingredients gently

SLICED RADISH FLOWERS

DORIS MOSS

the art of food presentation

Two radishes are needed to provide enough good slices for two five-petal blossoms. Halved cherry tomatoes are the centers and the ring around the rim. You may use the whole cherry tomato if it seems too small for cutting. However, it is desirable that the cherry tomatoes used be approximately of equal size for appearance. Green onions serve as the leaves and the stems. If you are not satisfied with the tone of the surface of the salad, try sprinkling on chopped chive.

POPPIES

Depending upon the size of your salad, one poppy shall need from three to five petals. Each petal is a slice from the surface of a fresh tomato done with a sharp knife cutting downward while the fruit rests upright. No more than three petals from one tomato ought to be attempted.

Right: View of tomato from top. Knife slices downward along dotted lines.

Scrape the meat away from each cut. What remains is an ideal petal because of its color, sturdiness, and curvature. The center of the poppy is represented by a slice of black olive taken from the olive in the same way that the petals were taken form the tomato. Green onions, cucumber peels, or both form leaves and stems. Numerous black olive peels circle the edge of the salad.

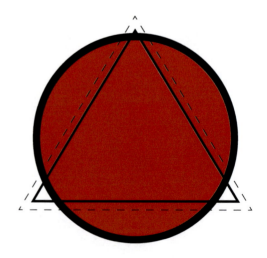

CHAPTER THREE
the salad bar

STAR FLOWERS

Create a star flower by cutting five or six even wedges from a fresh tomato and scraping off the meat. Arrange the wedges face down on the salad to form a star pattern. Make two such flowers for a large salad. Whole black olives are the centers of the blossoms. Green onion, cucumber peels, or both form leaves and stems. The star flowers may be artfully encircled by halved cucumber slices.

ROSE

A steak knife is the best utensil for this job. Begin by cutting out the bottom navel of a fresh and firm tomato. From the bottom peel the whole skin in a spiral manner in one continuous piece. shape the peel to make an imitation of a rose blossom. Do not worry; a little practice will make perfect results. Green onion, cucumber peels, or both are good for a stem and leaves. Halved slices of cucumber surround the salad and the rose while halved slices of tomato are in another ring just outside of the cucumber. Some chopped parsley may be added to perfect what is already a beautiful balance of green and dark red

DORIS MOSS
the art of food presentation

ROSE VARIATION

For a smaller preparation of potato salad or, perhaps, for individual servings you may choose to make one or more rose blossoms in the manner described above to be served without stems. make the blossom rest on green leaves cut form cucumber peels. A ready-to-eat outer boundary may be constructed of little cherry tomato halves or halved tomato slices with smaller halved slices of cucumber. Sprinkled chopped parsley is optional.

MUSHROOMS

If you were to come across mushrooms resembling these out in the wild, you had better keep your distance. These, however, will only poison any unjust reputation as a mediocre hostess you may have here fore acquired. These edible mushrooms are made from three whole hard-boiled eggs pressed fat side down into the potato salad. Each egg is capped by the shell of a half tomato which has had its seeds removed. An invisible toothpick extends from the bottom of the half tomato into the top of the egg for fastening. Little drops of mayonnaise are applied by a toothpick to the top of each mushroom for spots. A thick dose of chopped parsley is spread to suggest grass at the feet of the toadstools. Halved tomato slices surround the mushroom mound. One halved slice of hard-boiled egg lies on top of each halved tomato slice.

CHAPTER THREE
the salad bar

MACARONI SALADS

There is no need for your favorite macaroni salad to remain unadorned. Little effort is required to brighten its face. Try cutting pieces of American cheese and ham to form diamond shapes as we know them from playing cards. They may be arranged in an alternating ring as shown in the illustration, or by using your imagination you may create other patterns such as the star based upon diamond shape cuts we use on the cole slaw below. Finely chopped parsley should be sprinkled on top of the macaroni salad. Another plan for decorating your macaroni salad uses slices of hard-boiled egg in a ring around the edge. Over the yolk area of each slice of egg, one slice of a carrot is placed. Black olive peels rest where egg slices join. This last example could be used for a potato salad as well.

DORIS MOSS
the art of food presentation

COLE SLAW SALAD

For those of us who enjoy coleslaw I declare that bell pepper and carrot are in its best match for decoration. Make thin slices from the thicker end of a carrot. By making little V-shape cuts all around the carrot slice, you may create a carrot blossom like those in the two coleslaw decorations. Make a ring around the edge of the salad with bell pepper strips and carrot blossoms alternating. For the other illustrated example you will need to add lengthwise slices from a very thick carrot. make these slices into diamond shapes all of them of equal size. Seven diamonds can equal a great centerpiece star. Bell pepper strips make semi-circle enclosures for the carrot blossoms on the edge. These enclosures transform the entire surface of the coleslaw into a star or blossom theme depending upon how one sees it.

I include with the remaining salads in this chapter my recommended recipes for them. They are not as commonly used as coleslaw, green leaf tossed, macaroni, or potato salads, and you may wish to add them to your salad bar repertoire. Of course we never fail to decorate them.

CHAPTER THREE
the salad bar

MARINATED GREEN BEAN SALAD

Decorate the salad by surrounding it with alternating halved slices of onion and tomato.

- Frozen green beans
- Bottled Italian dressing
- Chopped bell peppers
- Chopped onions
- Chopped red pimentos
- A dash of garlic powder
- Sugar

PEA SALAD

- One lb. cooked frozen peas
- 1 tablespoon mayonnaise
- Diced red pimentos
- Onion salt
- White pepper
- A dash of garlic powder.

Make an egg daisy with the wedges from two hard-boiled eggs. One whole extracted yolk is the center of the blossom. A lace-like trim of halved egg slices encircles the salad.

DORIS MOSS
the art of food presentation

HERRING SALAD

- One eight-ounce jar of diced herring in sour cream
- One cup of diced dill pickle
- Three hard-boiled eggs diced
- One cup of diced apple
- Two cups of chopped onion
- One cup of mayonnaise

After mixing well all of the ingredients, refrigerate the salad and serve it cold. If you have the means to prepare your own fresh herring and sour cream to match the other ingredients, please do so. Onion slices and pairs of one larger with one smaller onion rings decorate the salad. The slices and rings are dipped in paprika.

CHAPTER THREE

the salad bar

MEAT SALAD

Use three cups of luncheon meat or of leftover meat cut to julienne strips. Add just enough Italian dressing to moisten the meat strips, then mix in the following ingredients.

- One cup mayonnaise
- One cup of halved onion rings
- One tablespoon of sweet pickle relish

Make conical hats out of slices of salami into each of which is placed a stuffed olive. These salami hats form a ring around the edge of the meat salad.

DORIS MOSS

the art of food presentation

CELERY SALAD

Cover one celery root with hot water, one-half cup white vinegar, and one tablespoon of flour. Cook until the root is soft. Cool, slice, and mix with the following ingredients.

- One cup of chopped onion
- One-half cup of chopped parsley
- One cup of bottled Italian dressing

Slice five wedges from a halved avocado and five wedges from a halved tomato. Form them to the shape of a pinwheel which revolves around one whole cherry tomato at the center of the surface of the salad. Smaller tomato wedges make a ring around the edge of the salad. The avocado and tomato pinwheel decoration would go well on a mixed bean salad too.

CHAPTER THREE
the salad bar

BEET SALAD

- One sixteen-ounces can of sliced beets
- One tablespoon of wine vinegar
- One teaspoon of sugar
- One-half teaspoon of salt
- One-half teaspoon of pepper
- One bay leaf
- Two cloves
- One medium-sized sliced onion

Save the beet juice from the can. Mix some of it with the ingredients, but save enough to stain the yolk areas of each of the sliced of hard-boiled egg that surround the salad. Sprinkle parsley on top of egg and salad.

DORIS MOSS
the art of food presentation

SPAGHETTI SALAD

- One pound of spaghetti broken in half and cooked
- Two cups mayonnaise
- Two teaspoons of mustard
- One teaspoon of sugar
- One teaspoon of salt
- One tablespoon of lemon juice or white vinegar
- One cup of chopped green onion
- One clove of garlic chopped
- Two hard-boiled eggs chopped
- One teaspoon of pepper

Form blossoms by laying five slices of carrot around both of the whole black olives. The stems are green onion. By splitting the green onion with a knife you may form leaves. Halved slices of carrot surround the salad. Sprinkle chive over all.

CHAPTER FOUR
main courses

In the preceding chapters we have created decorative dishes which may well have complemented the main course of any dinner. But what of the main course itself? If it is not necessary for you to serve your meat dish hot from the oven, you will find some wonderful displays of cold meat to consider in this chapter. Clearly, a hot, steaming dish has fewer options for success at very ornate decoration. Even so, don't let anything out of your kitchen undressed for the eye. A wide variety of naturally bright vegetable and spice additives from finely chopped parsley to paprika may embellish your hot meat. A perimeter of decorative fruit pieces may surround the meat on its platter or serving tray.

GLAZED HAM (CHAUD-FROID) - HOT OR COLD

One brilliant method of decorating meat, well known among professional culinary artists, is the preparation of a white glaze. For our first example a canned ham can be treated as follows:

- In a bowl dissolve two envelopes of unflavored gelatin and one cube of chicken bouillon in one half of a cup of hot water. Add approximately two cups of mayonnaise and stir.
- Remove a rack from your oven or perhaps use a barbecue grill and place the ham on it with a tray underneath the rack.
- Spread half of the glaze all over the ham except of course the bottom. Put the meat into the refrigerator to be chilled until the glaze is firm to the touch. Some of the glaze shall drip into the tray. While the first half of the glaze is in the refrigerator, the remainder while in one small pan should be placed into a larger pan of hot water to prevent the congealing of the glaze. After from five to ten minutes in the refrigerator, the ham comes out to be covered again by all of the remaining glaze. Again place the ham into the refrigerator with tray underneath until the glaze is firm to the touch.

Now a clear glaze is made to serve as a sort of glue to fasten the garniture which may be added. Furthermore, the clear glaze makes a shiny effect for such a showpiece meat. Dissolve one envelope of unflavored gelatin in a half cup of cold water. Add one cup of hot water.

DORIS MOSS
the art of food presentation

    You may decide to garnish your glazed ham as suggested by the illustration with mandarin oranges, maraschino cherries, peach, parsley, and lettuce, but remember that garnishing is an art which may express your creativity. Fruits in general make an excellent garniture for ham with parsley an ever useful and nutritious device for color contrast. Dip the selected fruit into the clear glaze briefly and only on the side that you intend to put down on the glazed ham. After the garniture is attached pour the clear glaze all over the glazed ham with a large spoon. The glazed ham should be returned to the refrigerator until all is firm to the touch once more. Allow from five to ten minutes.

    Transfer the glazed ham to a serving platter. Presumably you are more likely to prepare such a showpiece meat for a party as a part of a cold buffet. If so purchase another canned ham to be sliced evenly and arranged in a manner suggested by the illustration. One end of the glazed ham should be cut off to suggest to the imagination that the slices originate from the glazed whole. Be artful with the arrangement on the patter; do not heap the slices haphazardly.

THE GARNISHED TONGUE

    Purchase two fresh unsmoked whole tongues. One is to be sliced and arranged around the other that you garnish. Prepare a clear glaze in the same amount and manner as described for the glazed ham chaud-froid. The purpose again is to fasten the garniture and to make the tongue glisten. For a suitable garniture to this unusual and dimly colored dish, I recommend sliced hard-boiled egg in a row all along the tongue with diamond shaped cuts from black olive peels and radish peels alternating on top of the egg as illustrated.

CHAPTER FOUR
main courses

As with the glazed ham the bottoms of the pieces of garniture are dipped into the clear glaze before being laid on the tongue. Spoon the remainder of the clear glaze over all. Radish flowers with parsley decorate the perimeter on top of the slices. These radish flowers are made by cutting of the top, then carving four times into the radish all around without cutting pieces off.

THE TUNA DISH

Prepare your favorite tuna salad from about four regular cans of tuna. On your serving tray form the tuna salad to make the shape of a fish. The texture of the tuna salad should not be too wet for shaping. Garnish the tuna on top with flower shapes made from black olive peels with a cherry tomato in the center. A stuffed olive is a fine eye for the fish. The tuna swims in a wave of finely shredded lettuce surrounded by thinly sliced tomato wedges. Two suggestions for further decoration of the tuna are deviled eggs and an escort of penguins. Complete instructions for the eggs were given in chapter two and the creation of the penguins is found in chapter five.

DORIS MOSS
the art of food presentation

COLD SALMON PLATTER

Mix a half cut of water, a half cup of white wine, one sliced carrot, one quartered onion, one bay leaf, a few sprigs of parsley, two or three peppercorns, and one teaspoon of salt. Boil this mixture and then simmer it for ten minutes. Strain the mixture through a sieve. Pour this broth all over a fresh salmon resting on a baking pan. The salmon selected ought to be young and not large. Steam this salmon in the oven at about three hundred and seventy-five degrees Fahrenheit from five to ten minutes. We do not want the fish to become tender; it must come out while yet firm to the touch. Allow the steamed salmon to cool at room temperature until all heat expires.

Carefully remove the steamed salmon from the baking pan to a serving platter. Scrape away from one side the black skin between the gills and the tail. You may decorate the flayed area with halved egg slices and halved radish peels as suggested by the illustration. Dissolve one envelope of unflavored gelatin in half cup of cold water. Add one cup of hot water. Apply this clear glaze all over the salmon. The glaze will fasten the garniture, give a shine, and retard spoiling. You may decorate the area of the latter in front of the salmon with lemon, tomato wedges, and king crab meat on a bed of finely shredded lettuce. A crown may be carved from a lemon and attached to the head of the salmon with a toothpick not visible from where diners will be admiring your work.

TRAYS OF CHEESES AND COLD CUTS

The remaining examples of this chapter require a minimum of labor but can complement as the main course any elements of chapters one, two, and three as well as to serve as trimming for larger fiestas. Even a more humble presentation of common cold cuts can be enhanced by your method of arrangement. Fold each cold cut once and place it in groups of its own kind to form alternating circles around the serving tray. A carved tomato star with parsley is the axis in the illustrated example.

CHAPTER FOUR
main courses

Symmetry attracts the eye. You may discover that the more care you take to present your tray attractively results in greater consumption by your guests. However, do not overload the tray at the beginning; be prepared to replenish.

The cheese tray gives a vertical contrast from the circular theme preceding. Two rows of alternating triangular slices of American and Swiss cheese flank a column of assorted cheese chunks equipped with toothpicks. A scarlet apple and dark grapes give a contrast to the light colored cheese.

DELICATESSEN ASSORTMENT

A visit to the delicatessen may produce a fancier assortment of cold cuts. Listed in order from the top of the illustrated tray are rows of smoked ham, cooked ham, salami garnished with pickle, gelbwurst or yellow sausage, and blood tongue. A large cut of about two pounds of pastrami heads the field. The pastrami is garnished with cherry tomatoes fastened by toothpicks. Sprigs of parsley complete a beautiful feast for the eye.

COLD OPEN-FACED SANDWICHES

For some occasions cold open-faced sandwiches may serve as a main course deserving embellishment. The two outside rows on the illustrated tray are slices of French bread topped with mayonnaise, hard-boiled egg slices, anchovy, and stuffed olive slices. Inside of these are rows of pumpernickel and cream cheese sandwiches.

Lay on a slice of pumpernickel a matching slice of cream cheese to be topped in turn with another slice of pumpernickel. Repeat this procedure twice in order to make three layers of cheese. Press slightly and then quarter the sandwich. Two sandwiches quartered provide for two rows. Swiss cheese may substitute for the cream cheese if you prefer.

DORIS MOSS
the art of food presentation

Next in line are triangles of buttered whole wheat bread covered by matching triangles of American cheese. Smaller triangles of Swiss cheese now take their places to be capped in turn by tiny triangles cut from black olive peel.

In the center is a row of halved slices of buttered rye bread. Each slice is covered by a matching slice of liverwurst. By cutting a dill pickle into halves and with both halves cutting slits, which do not detach any parts, you may open pickle fans. These fans along with pimento strips make a delightful garniture for the tops of the liverwurst sandwiches.

HOT OPEN-FACED SANDWICHES

A tray of grilled sandwiches for light dinners of unexpected guests can also be made attractive to the eye as well as to the nose with some decorative technique. The following are just a few examples of the many little extra efforts you may try for hot food. Whatever is chosen to decorate a particular sandwich is meant to complement the flavor too.

Mexican Toast

Before grilling, the buttered toast is topped by green chilies and smothered by jack cheese. Two tomato slices and a bit of parsley are chosen for decoration.

Hamburger Toast

Fry your preferred ground beef and season it with onion salt, pepper, and barbecue seasoning. Cover the buttered toast with the meat and decorate with two triangles of American cheese and with mushrooms before grilling.

Wiener Toast

Spread catsup and mustard on an English muffin. Split a wiener in halves lengthwise and top it with strips of American cheese. Grill in on the English muffin.

Liver Toast

Fry one slice of calf's liver with onion rings and two rings of sliced apple seeds removed. Place the fried liver on buttered toast and season with salt and pepper. Lay the two slices of American cheese on top and garnish with the fried apple and onion rings before grilling.

Tuna Toast

Your favorite tuna salad is smothered by two layers of muenster cheese before it is grilled on buttered toast.

CHAPTER FIVE

especially for children...but not exclusively

Children appreciate food decoration and it encourages their enthusiastic consumption of dishes familiar or new. The youngsters have that lovable capacity for delight at some of our simplest devices. To gain their fascination you may need to apply your creativity. Your chances of encouraging children to try new things shall be much improved if you appeal to their fascination for make believe and to their sight.

If you have trouble getting your children to eat vegetables, the following two suggestions might help. Do your children have a favorite dip? Why not replace the plebian potato chip with bite-sized pieces of raw vegetable? Acquaint them with bell pepper, carrot, cauliflower, celery, cucumber, green onion, raw potato, radish, tomato, turnip, and zucchini by cutting pieces which may be applied to the dip. Arrange the various pieces to make an attractive formation around the dip by accentuating their contrasting colors. Naturally, if you prefer, large combinations are not necessary. One vegetable may be selected to accompany a dip when the taste pleases the consumer so well. Vegetable finger food with dip is an excellent idea for adult parties too. An idea to encourage children to eat cooked vegetables is to make attractive onion cups. Each large onion will make two cups. Peel and halve the onions and cook them in one inch of boiling, salted water until they are tender. Remove each center portion and fill with green peas, spinach, or broccoli. Top the filled onion cups with butter and sprinkle them with grated Cheddar cheese. Bake the cups about ten minutes.

THE VEGETABLE PLATTER

A vegetable dish with their favorite dip may persuade children to eat vegetables.

There are numerous visual stunts for helping children to enjoy wholesome food. Try serving mashed potatoes with an ice cream scoop or shaping rice with molding cups. Shave carrots to make curls. A celery stalk begs to be filled with peanut butter. Your children may enjoy the variety of simple geometric designs which may result from the way a slice of bread or complete sandwich is cut. Bright food items may be used to make flower shapes to top cereal, pudding, or jello. Previous chapters of this book should provide ample inspiration, if needed, for flower design. Cucumber may become either a boat or an airplane. By scooping out a cucumber in canoe fashion, cherry or strawberry passengers can be accommodated. A long strip shaved from the top of a cucumber can become the wing for an airplane by fitting it through slits. A propeller is made by pinning two small strips from the cucumber together as an X. The toothpick which is the pin of the X attaches the propeller to the nose of the cucumber plane.

DORIS MOSS

the art of food presentation

SMILEY

As the title of this chapter states, the ideas I present to you are not necessarily for children only. Smiley, for example, makes his appearance occasionally at the restaurant where I work and never fails to amuse all who are present. And yet he is such a simple fellow. Although an appropriate guest at a children's party, Smiley

smiles as well where minors are prohibited. Why don't you bring Smiley into your home? Just make your favorite macaroni and cheese salad and cover it with shredded yolk from hard-boiled eggs. The eyes are black olives. Black olive peels form the desired expression. Grated cheese may substitute for the shredded yolk.

The Smiley theme can be extended to homemade pizza or plain frozen pizza from the store.

Allow the children to design the face using salami slices and black olive peels on a thick bed of cheese. Other bright, contrasting food items that will go well with the pizza and oven temperatures may be equally suitable.

Here follow two complete meals for children which illustrate the essence of this chapter. notice the bright and contrasting colors. Notice also that nutrition is not sacrificed.

CHAPTER FOUR
especially for children...but not exclusively

THE LITTLE BREAD HOUSE

The house is constructed of buttered pumpernickel, painted with two different kinds of cheese, and garnished with peels of black olive and radish. Outside stands a flower of a whole cherry tomato on a celery stalk. A dish of cottage cheese is garnished with a flower of orange sections with a maraschino cherry and parsley in the center. When in season a strawberry or fresh cherry may substitute for the maraschino cherry. A scooped out tomato half is filled with celery and carrot sticks with radish flowers.

THE LADY BUGS

After cooking a cup and a half of rice, mix in well an eight-ounce can of tomato paste. Place rice ball on plate with a large ice cream scoop. One whole giant black olive is each head. Shaped black olive peels are the spots and antennas. Cook frozen green peas for the background. Serve fried chicken drumsticks with paper rosettes on an adjacent dish. The usual radish flower with parsley accentuates the green and red theme of the lady bug dish..

DORIS MOSS

the art of food presentation

THE PENGUINS

Now we become better acquainted with the penguins whom we met alongside the tuna in Chapter Four. Needless to say, the wonderful ideas for using these birds to decorate a dish are legion. Use hard-boiled eggs and giant black olives. A small slice from the bottom allows an egg to stand fat side down. The slice from the bottom ought to be egg white only, small dabs of which make the eyes of each penguin. Slice a small cavity on both sides to insert arms of olive peel. Fasten one whole giant olive for the head with a toothpick which stays invisible. A batch of clear glaze made as done in chapter four should be spooned over the entire penguin, Put each completed penguin into the refrigerator immediately from five to ten minutes.

One more important piece of garniture for children which is often neglected is your smile and pleasant manner when serving. When being routinely served by a cross parent who does not like the bother, a child may not wish to bother to eat well.

CHAPTER SIX

holiday ensembles

We have extra incentive to host and to prepare a decorative table when holidays arrive. To put you in the spirit of those occasions we will consider in detail a few appropriate ensembles for certain traditional holidays.

RAINBOW GELATIN LAYER DESSERT

You can make a rainbow of gelatin layer dessert. This dessert is a colorful creation which can decorate the table for any holiday. It is an excellent center piece as well as a dessert. Each layer represents the full contents of one six-ounce package of gelatin dessert. Dissolve the contents of the package in two cups of boiling water. Slowly add enough vanilla ice cream stirred until all melted, to equal three and one-half cups of mixture. Pour this mixture into a glass loaf pan. Chill the gelatin layer until it has set but is not quite firm. When the next layer is added it should already have become slightly thickened, but not enough to prevent it from pouring smoothly on top of the first layer. Be sure to chill each layer until it has set but is not firm before adding the next layer. This will prevent the layers from slipping apart.

Although the process is simple it is a time consuming process. The package of gelatin dessert should be prepared one and a time. I suggest that your prepare this dessert one day ahead of the occasion when you serve it. Leave it in the refrigerator overnight. When you are ready to serve it, submerge the entire loaf pan briefly in hot water long enough only to notice the water seeping down the edge of the glass loaf pan. This loosens the gelatin dessert from the pan allowing you to turn the pan upside down on your serving platter and leaving behind a ready and colorful dessert. As was true of the hors d'oeuvres a mirror may be a very effective alternative to a fancier serving tray for this colorful dessert. The top layer of the rainbow gelatin layer dessert, that is the first layer in the loaf pan, should be of a soft color allowing you to decorate the top with a row of whipped cream mounds applied by a pastry bag and tube. Place a maraschino cherry on top of each mound. Mint leaves lie between the mounds. Halved pineapple rings may surround the gelatin dessert. Top each halved pineapple ring with a wedge of mandarin orange. The selection of flavors for the rainbow gelatin layer dessert may be made according to the thematic colors of a given holiday. However, any rainbow will brighten your table for any occasion.

Your heavily drinking guests and your heavy schedule may best be accommodated by a light buffet on New Year's. Here is an ensemble to meet your requirements during the happy occasion of changing calendars.

DORIS MOSS

the art of food presentation

FUNNY FACES, ROLLMOPS, AND KING NEPTUNE'S SALAD

Funny Faces

Decorate hard-boiled eggs to make funny faces. The faces are peels of black olives and radishes glued on by clear glaze. The hats are all fastened by invisible toothpicks and are from natural source materials such as tomato, radish, cherry tomato, carrot, salami, and orange rind. Stand these characters on a bed of shredded lettuce. There are numerous creative ideas possible for making funny faces. They may be thematic for a certain holiday. Also, they are ideal guests at a children's party.

Rollmops

Surround a molded tomato aspic with rollmops from the delicatessen on a bed of chopped aspic. To prepare the tomato aspic dissolve one six-ounce package of lemon flavored gelatin and one teaspoon of onion slat in two cups of hot tomato juice. Add a cup and a half of cold tomato juice and one tablespoon of Worchestershire sauce. Pour this mixture into your mold and allow it to chill until it is firm. To prepare the chopped aspic dissolve one envelope of unflavored gelatin in one-half cup of cold water. Add one cup of hot bouillon from one beef cube. Stir this mixture in a pie plate and then allow it to harden in the refrigerator. Chop the cooled aspic to fine chunks. Sprinkle it slightly with sherry to prevent the chunks from sticking together.

CHAPTER SIX
holiday ensembles

KING NEPTUNE'S NEW YEAR SALAD

In a large bowl mix the following ingredients:

- One cup of baby shrimps
- One cup of crab meat
- One cup of cooked and flaked sole, turbot, or lobster
- Two cups of chopped celery
- One-half cup of finely chopped onion
- Three tablespoons of fresh lemon juice
- One tablespoon of dillweed
- A dash of garlic powder
- One and one-half cups of mayonnaise
- Salt and pepper to taste

FESTIVE FOOD FOR EASTER

Garnish the salad with wedges of hard-boiled eggs and wedges of cherry tomatoes alternating in a ring with faces down around the rim. Dabs of caviar nestle between the wedges. Chopped parley make a ring inside of the wedges.

A roasted leg of lamb with trimming, a cottage cheese and fruit salad, and a special chocolate egg comprises our example of an Easter ensemble. Colors are soft but bright to match the atmosphere of Spring. Decorate the surface of the lamb roast with a tulips design cut out of lemon and tomato peels. Use cucumber peels for stems and leaves. Surround the roast with apple baskets filled with mint jelly.

To make apple baskets peel large apples and cut off their polar regions. Scoop out a small hollow for the filling in each with a knife. Press downward on each apple with a circular zigzag cookie cutter. In a pot barely cover the apple baskets with cold water. Cut two lemons in halves and after squeezing some of their juice into the pot add them into the water. The lemon serves to prevent the apple baskets from turning brown. Bring the contents in the pot to a boil. Remove the apple baskets from the hot liquid with a sieve and allow them to cool.

DORIS MOSS

the art of food presentation

The cottage cheese is garnished with five pinwheel formations of mandarin orange sections. Each pinwheel revolves around a maraschino cherry. Pieces of pineapple ring of equal size surround the pinwheels. Sprigs of parsley or fresh mint leaves are added for color contrast between pinwheels. You may also use fresh peeled kiwi fruit sliced to form a beautiful flower.

An ornate chocolate egg can be easily constructed in your Easter table. The egg consists of two hollow halves made separately. With shortening you can make a mold which is the shape of half of an egg. Cover the molded shortening with two layers of foil. From a package of semi-sweet chocolate chips place eight one-ounce squares in a small container which in turn is placed in hot water just long enough for the squares to melt. Remove the container from the hot water and stir the chocolate until it is completely melted. Semi-sweet chocolate tends to hold its shape until stirred. Now with a spatula cover the top layer of foil with the melted chocolate. Allow the chocolate to harden in the refrigerator. The foil makes it possible for the half egg shell to be easily extracted from the mold. On the same mold make the other half of the chocolate egg by repeating the above process. You may have creative fun decorating your chocolate Easter egg with a pastry bag and tube.

Can it be that fresh ideas are still possible for the Christmas table? From the following you may find something novel to blend with your Yuletide tradition.

GLAZED HAM CHAUD-FROID

Prepare a glazed ham chaud-froid as detailed in chapter four. For a variation of its top garniture use halved orange slices with the usual maraschino cherries and parsley sprigs. Surround the glazed ham with baskets carved from grapefruit. Each scooped out grapefruit may be filled with grapes and a single maraschino cherry and parsley sprig for a seasonal touch.

CHAPTER SIX
holiday ensembles

Below you'll find recipes for various festive presentations:

AMBROSIA SALAD

- Drain a two and one-half ounce can of mandarin oranges
- Two and one-half ounce can of fruit cocktail; mix them together
- Two cups of whipping cream
- One-half cup coconut flakes.

Sprinkle coconut flakes all over the top. Garnish the rim with mint flavored maraschino cherries alternating with regular maraschino cherries. Slice some canned pear halves evenly and dip the slices into the liquid from the jar of the mint flavored cherries. Arrange a star or pinwheel shape with the dipped pear slices and put a regular maraschino cherry in the center.

FESTIVE SHRIMP SALAD

Combine in a bowl the following:

- Two cups of untanned baby shrimps from the meat department
- One-half of a cup of finely chopped onion
- One-half of a cup of mayonnaise
- One tablespoon of fresh lemon juice
- One teaspoon of dillweed
- Salt and pepper to taste

Garnish the top with chopped parsley in a ring to resemble a Christmas wreath. Cut strips from canned pimento halves to form a ribbon. Bits of pimento make berries. Of course the festive shrimp salad can be very festive for occasions other than Christmas with a decoration other than the wreath. Halved slices of lemon surround the edge of the salad.

CHRISTMAS FRUIT TRAY

From the outside inward in rows:

- Single grapes dipped in egg white, then rolled in powdered sugar.
- Canned peach halves dried on a paper towel, then filled by a pastry bag and tube with a mixture of two three-ounce pack-ages of cream cheese softened by triple sec liquor, and finally topped with a maraschino cherry.
- Canned pear halves fried and stuffed in the same manner with a mixture of one three-ounce package of cream cheese, one teaspoon of fresh lemon juice, and enough grenadine for pink color topped by sprigs of parsley.
- Canned pineapple rings are topped by whole canned prunes.

DORIS MOSS
the art of food presentation

MOLDED STRAWBERRY GELATIN DESSERT

Prepare in a circular mold a strawberry flavor gelatin dessert. Form a pinwheel of canned peach slices on the top of the mold. At Christmas time the pinwheel can revolve around a sprig of holly. Sprinkle coconut flakes over the remainder of the mold. This gelatin dessert is encircled by a ring of peach slices and coconut flakes.

VEGETABLE FLOWER BOUQUET CENTERPIECES

You can impress your guests and draw form nature's bounty by sculpting an exquisite vegetable flower bouquet. Not only will your vegetable bouquet convey your warm hospitality, but it can become a delicious taste treat as well.

Since all of the food and the centerpiece can be prepared in advance you can relax and enjoy being the hostess for a great occasion your guests will long remember.

Food sculpting is an ancient art form long practiced in the oriental culture. Baskets make wonderful containers for vegetable centerpieces, as do large, hollowed vegetables as melons and squashes. I recommend packing your container tightly with bunches of fresh parsley because it holds up well and provides an attractive green background. You also can use leaves from leeks.

To prepare the parsley, remove the rubber bands from one bunch at a time, working each bunch into an evenly rounded bouquet. Pull out any conspicuous stems and reposition them at the side of the bunch. Replace the rubber bands and, if necessary, trip the parsley bunches into more evenly rounded shapes. Pack the container tightly with the trimmed bunches so the skewered vegetable flowers will stand in place when inserted. The parsley filled container can be prepared a day ahead and misted with cool water. Make sure the base of your vegetable container is flat on the bottom. Cover the flower stem (the bamboo skewer) with green onion leaves.

CHAPTER SIX
holiday ensembles

Useful Items - oriental bamboo skewers, bowl of ice water, kitchen scissors, cookie cutters, paring knife, paper towels, toothpicks, vegetable peeler, large knife and melon baller.

Instructions for Making Vegetable Flower
Cut thin slices of large carrots or turnips. Cut the slices into floral shapes using assorted shaped cutters (for food) - white flower shapes can be dyed with beet juice. Different colors and shapes can be used together to form an assortment of flowers.

Chili Flowers
Carefully cut green or red chili pepper into eights using kitchen scissors or a paring knife. Do not cut through the stem end. Drop into water at least overnight for petals to bloom.

Spider Lily
For small lily use a green onion, for a large lily, use a leek. Make a carrot ball by pushing a melon bailer down into the carrot and then twisting. Cut through 3-4 inches of leek stems. When you finish, the leek should look shredded, but with all shreds attached the end. Open up the leek and push the carrot ball with a toothpick into the center. Submerge in cool water until ready to use.

Hawaiian Flower
Use red bell pepper. With kitchen shears, cut vegetable into a heart shape. Place the heart on a skewer and top with a baby corn.

Radish Flowers
With a paring knife, cut into the radish to create a flower.

Fantasy Flower
Slice thin petals from white turnips. Roll one petal up tight. Arrange petals overlapping around the turnip roll. Hold the flower together with toothpicks.

Lotus Blossoms
Use green or red cabbage leaves. Using kitchen shears, cut petal shapes from the stem end of the cabbage leaf. Make sure that the cupped side is up. On the underside, shave any thickness away with a sharp knife. Push a carrot slide into skewer, push on the petals one by one and top with a carrot ball. Position the petals in a circle.

Onion Flower
Remove the outer skin from small-medium sized red or white onions. Using a paring knife, cut V-shaped all the way through. Hold the onion under hot running water and separate the onion flowers. Various centers can be inserted.

I hope you'll enjoy utilizing the presented suggestions and illustrations. Some unheard ideas are waiting for you to be created. Apply your own creative ideas. Satisfied will be the stomach; gratified will be the eye.

~ HAVE FUN ~

ABOUT THE AUTHOR

Ms. Moss has been hired to avail her European culinary expertise and personal creativity for a number of renown Fine Dining room and Casino Buffets in Nevada for many years. She has trained numerous assistant employees in the skills of aesthetic food presentation. She herself is a fanatic for utilizing natural ingredients in food decorating and an ardent advocate for the "health food" movement.

Presently she is affiliated with various organizations and catering groups organizing buffets and providing beautifully presented platters for special banquets and private parties. The book is especially helpful and educational for all who are engaged or interested in the art of food preparation.

Made in the USA
Las Vegas, NV
04 December 2023